SPECTRALS
IN
OMEGA

SPECTRALS IN OMEGA

JAY SNODGRASS
2015

© 2015 Hysterical Books
Tallahassee, FL
Thomasville, GA

ISBN 978-1511715836

The production of this book was made possibile by
a residency at tthe Thomasville Center for the Arts,
Thomasville GA. 2015.

For Kristine

SPECTRALS

IN

OMEGA

The glass is permanent like a tomb
wherein you see yourself looking, laughing
deranged, posed on the piano, or the resuscitated
armoire where the spiders keep their night clothes.

The mouth is moving, asking to be taken
on a date, to be furloughed to the wind.

There is an array of antique fans displayed,
they hide the mouths of the besought women, the suitor's object,
the secret quivering like a moth's wings, on and on
in the dark.

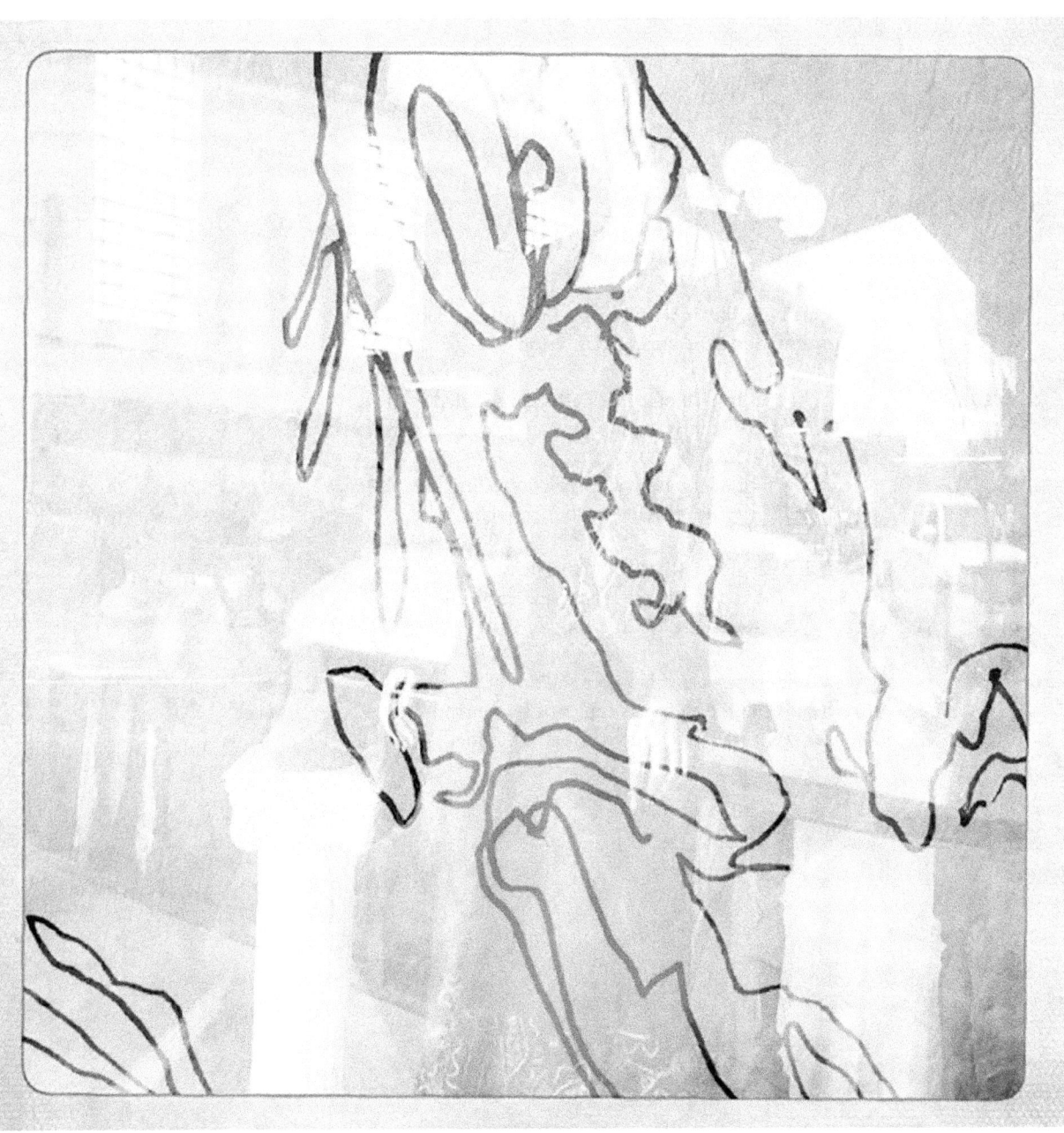

One bulb, lilly in a flowerbox, up in the creaking
disputations, the creaking anterior

of houses in disrepair, like coffins, paralleled in glass.
I'm infernal and watching the sun grow across the lawn.

Every face is a quarter, a mind-controlling fungus spore
traveling in the currents of your thought.

Mind-shadows, what you thought you knew
just beyond the curve in the road, responding
to your appearance with crow-flight,

a sudden passage that raises the dog's
head from the cadaver's trail, not human, but logical,
the scent trail of a decayed frog in the road.

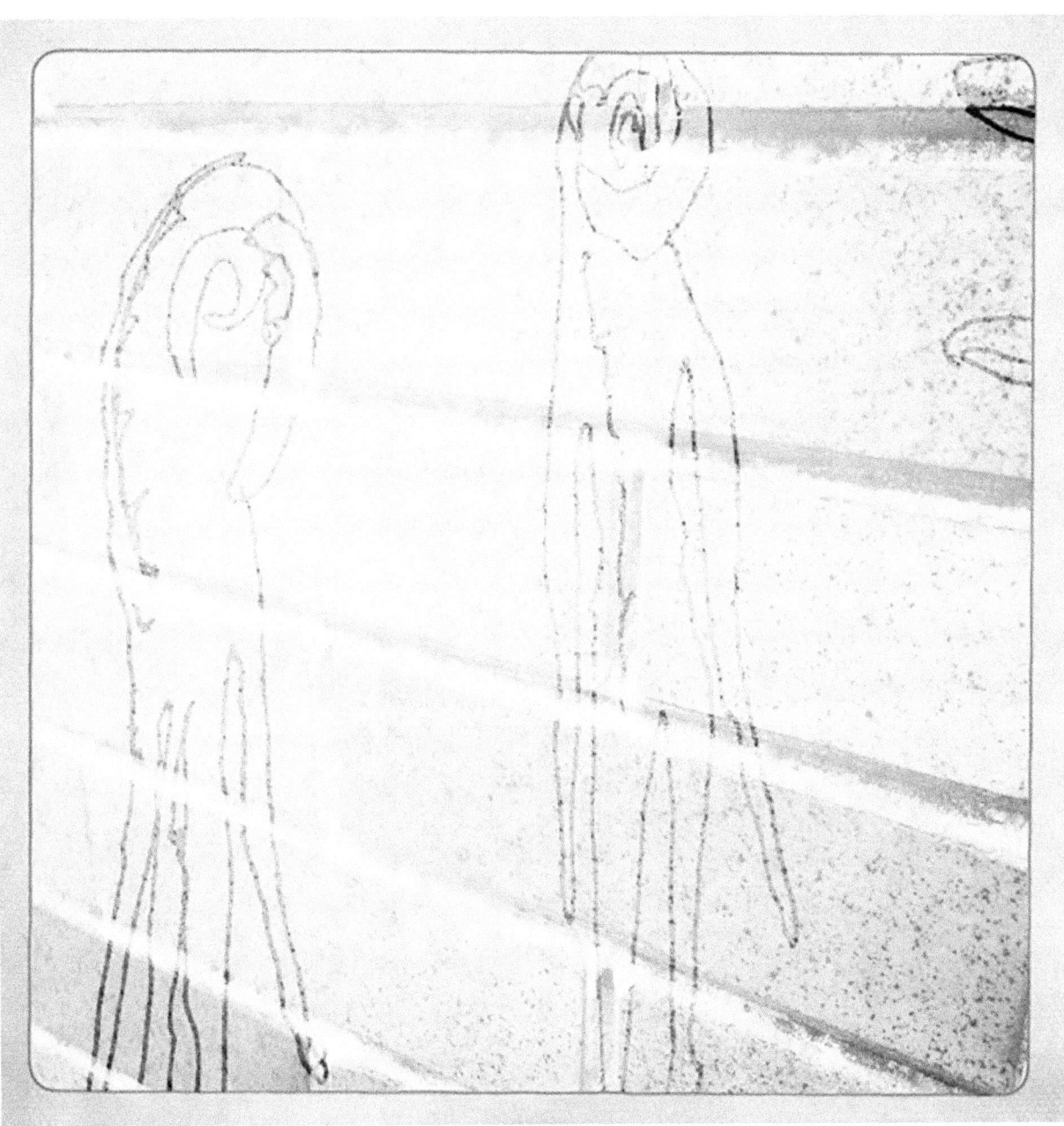

I recall the phone
unwinding, the vine of its twisted ear
burrowing into my soft grey matter.

Grains of the neck where the twist of a neck tie
pulls a business shadow down like a movie shade,
a blind white field reshapes the wall, tendrils
of smoke in the concentrated light.

There's a railing. Psychic echo of hands
sliding, stabilizing, crooked righting
the bones in history's resetting.

Often a tree will call out a hairdo,
theew will be a shimmer of passing on the sidewalk,
memory paste holding the deteriorating city together.

Peace among the wildflowers, purple
and swollen for an afternoon.

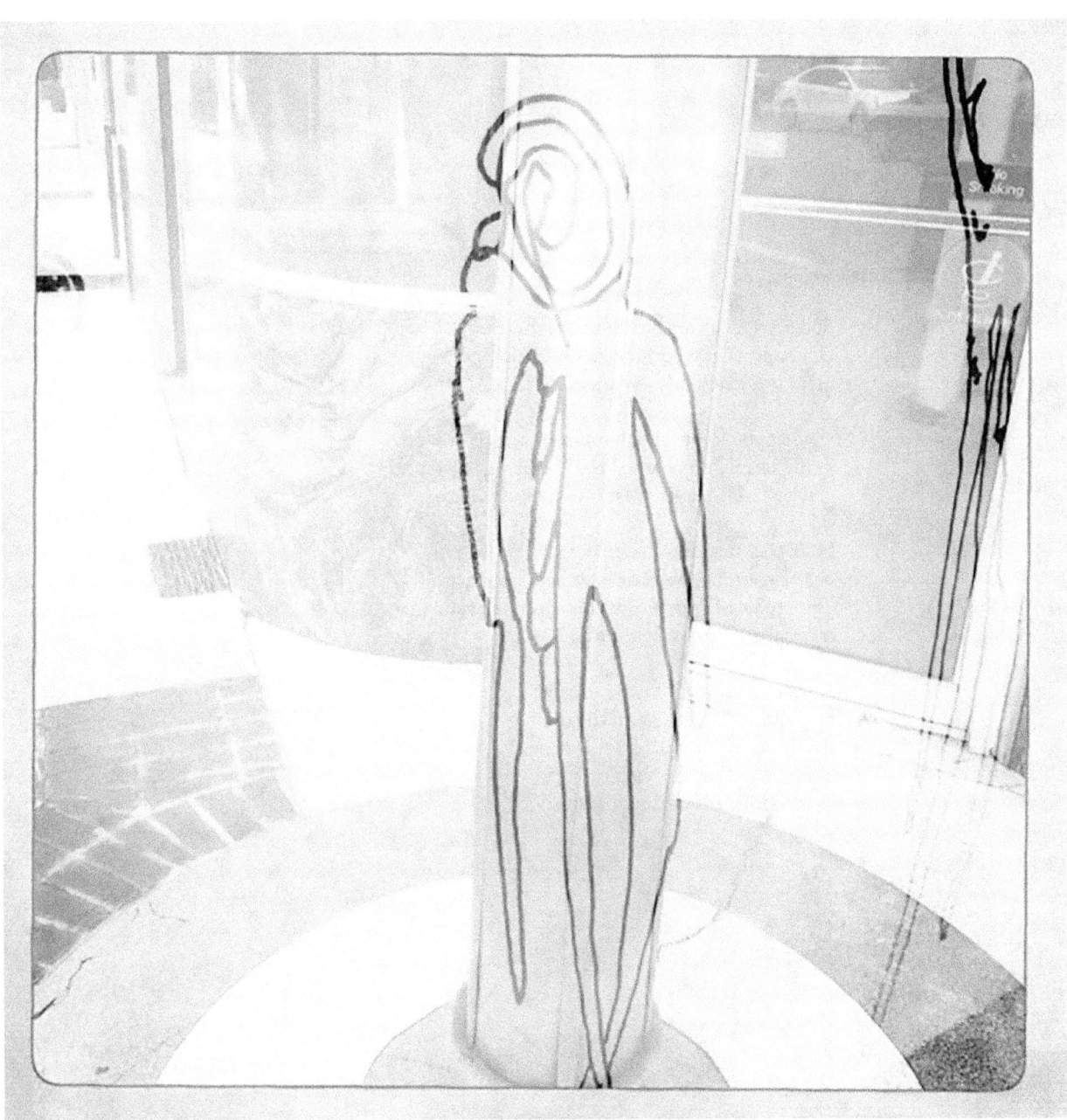

Super swollen cars berate the highway.
Under arms of wild flowers turn pale faces
up to sudden winds. Ashamed to look

at what you know about yourself fading
in the headlamp's dark glass. The passages around
gravity's well, surging, escaping, twisted.

Industrial shadows make secrets
out of yearning, we wait with tires on gravel.
The needle of your words press into my skin
remembering passages and hiding.

And the glaze on the sale sticker
meditates its marriage to the dulling
train rail, the thundercloud worries
like a proud father. No one can buy
the shadows off of their dreams.

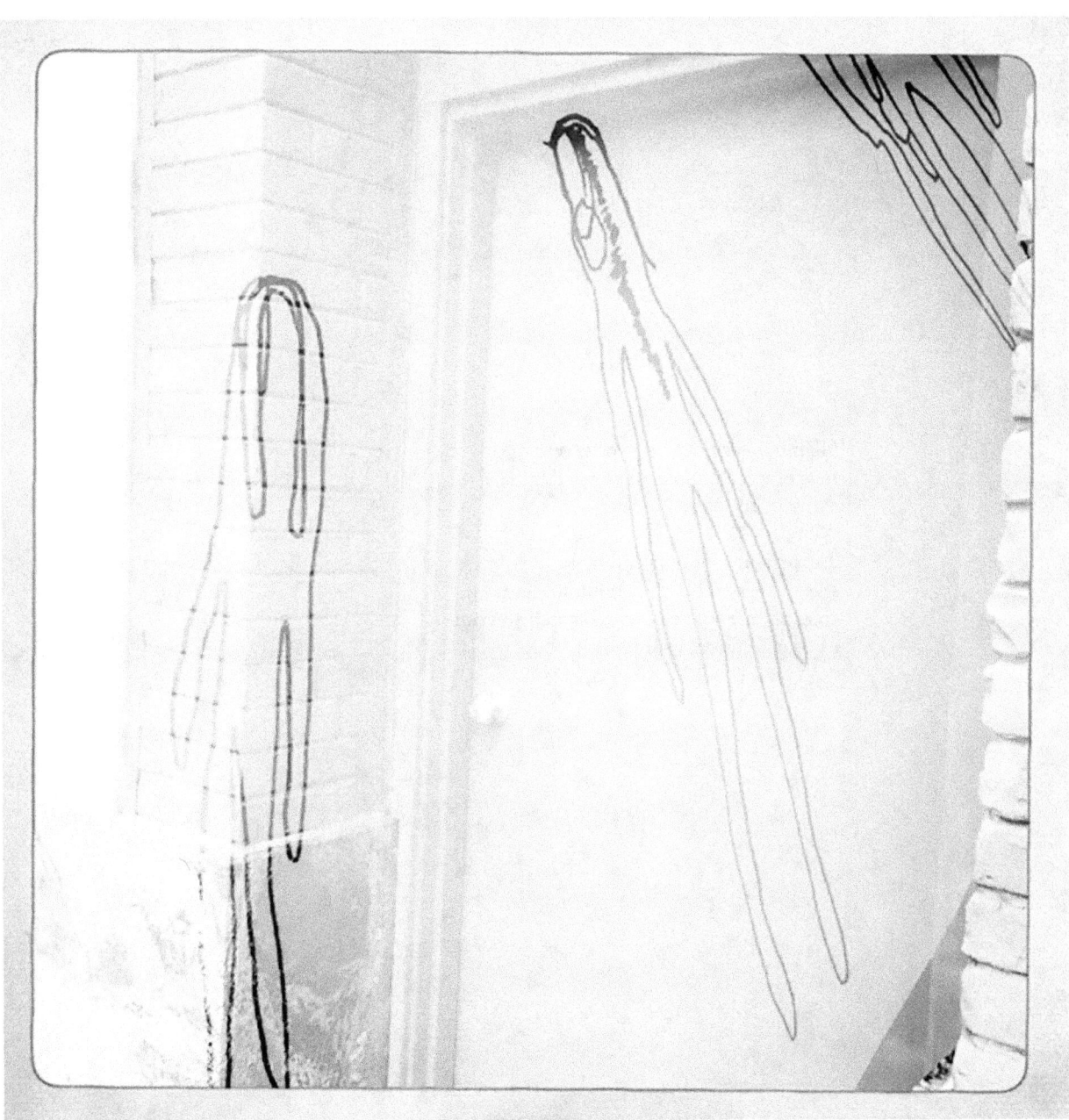

Glamour corrodes into yesteryear,
tiers of waxed linoleum worried by so
many worn soles.

The pressures of unfashionable
shoes, weary echo of a grandmother floor,
creaking her sore elbows to snatch you out
of your delusion, your reverie.

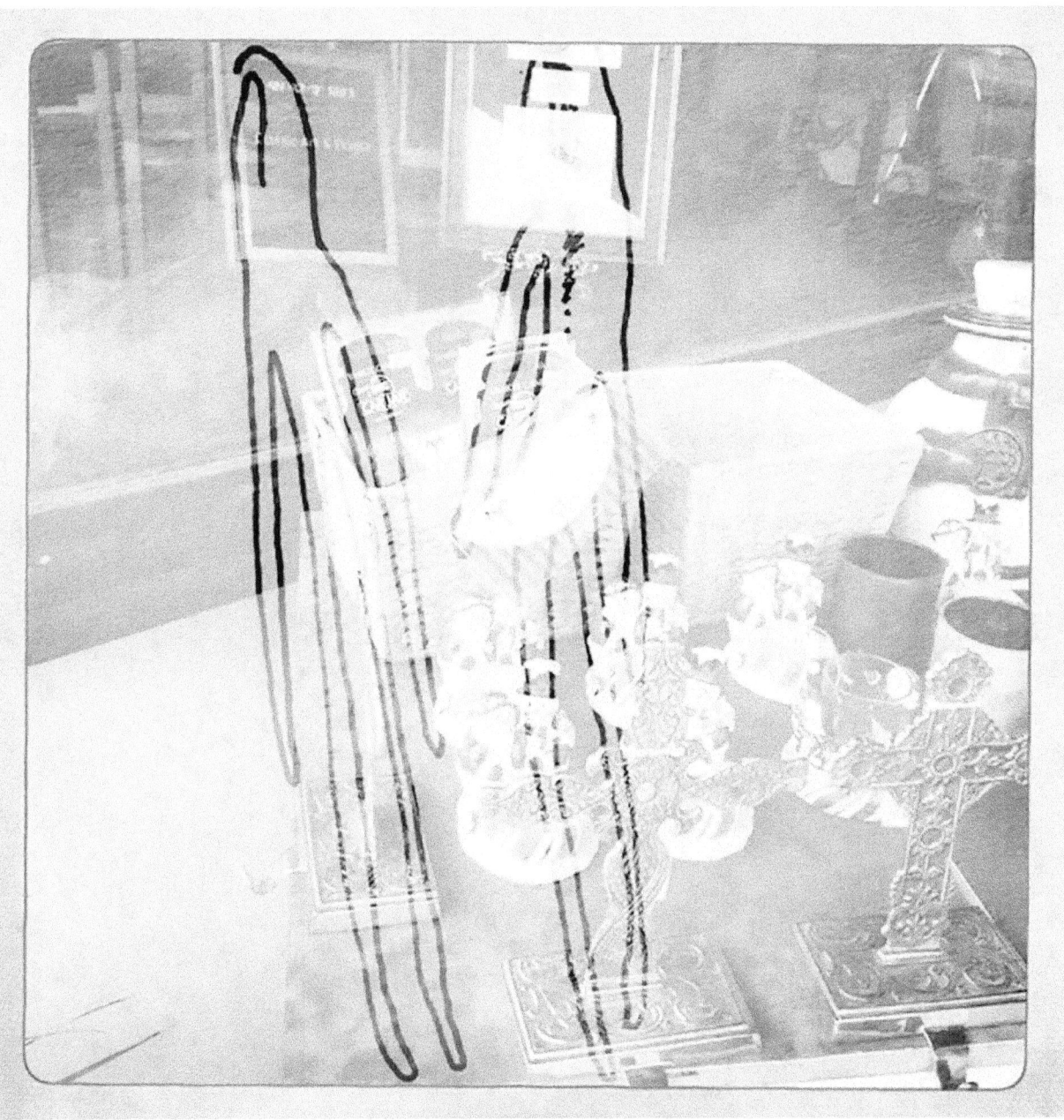

Here's how eternity unbuckles:
after the car went over the rail,
after the airplane flooded with immoveable
pressure, after the train cars
shook hands in a halfmile rumble
and the Yardman's fingers let go
their cargo of touches, passengers,
the hard crease of buttons, a creature's
pelt, soft blouses slipped up
right. Here's how the shadow greets you:
with a patient waiver like leaves
in the wind outside your window,
gently trying to get your attention
to tell you not to go inside, never go.

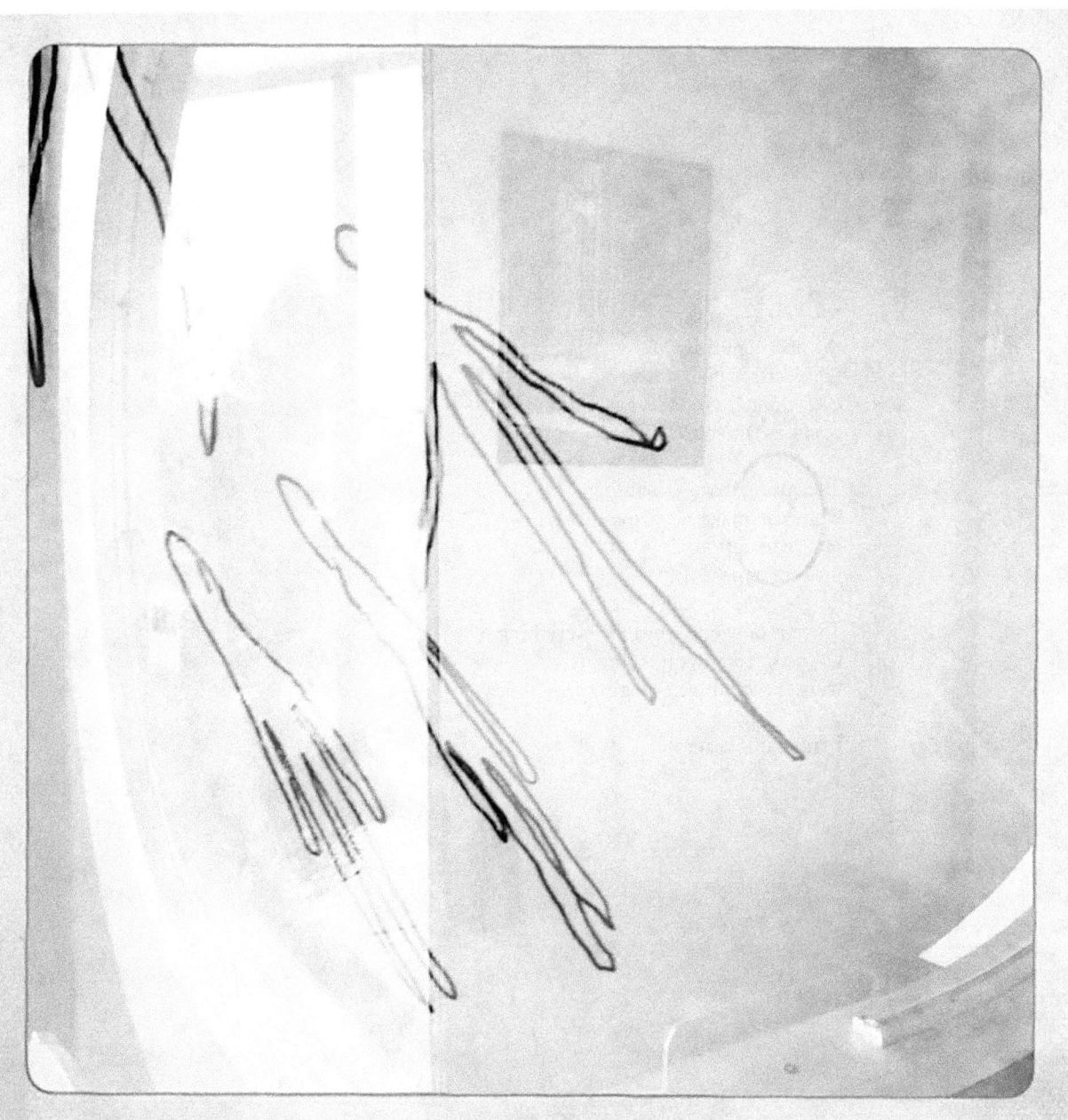

Every step across
the floating bridge,
thespectral canal,
everything is crooked, every move
confuses the spirits.

They turn after you, sniffing
while you make new cross roads
into redemption
into embryo.

There is only one word for everything
but no one knows it, knows it
will set everything straight.

I know this is across
where I am not.

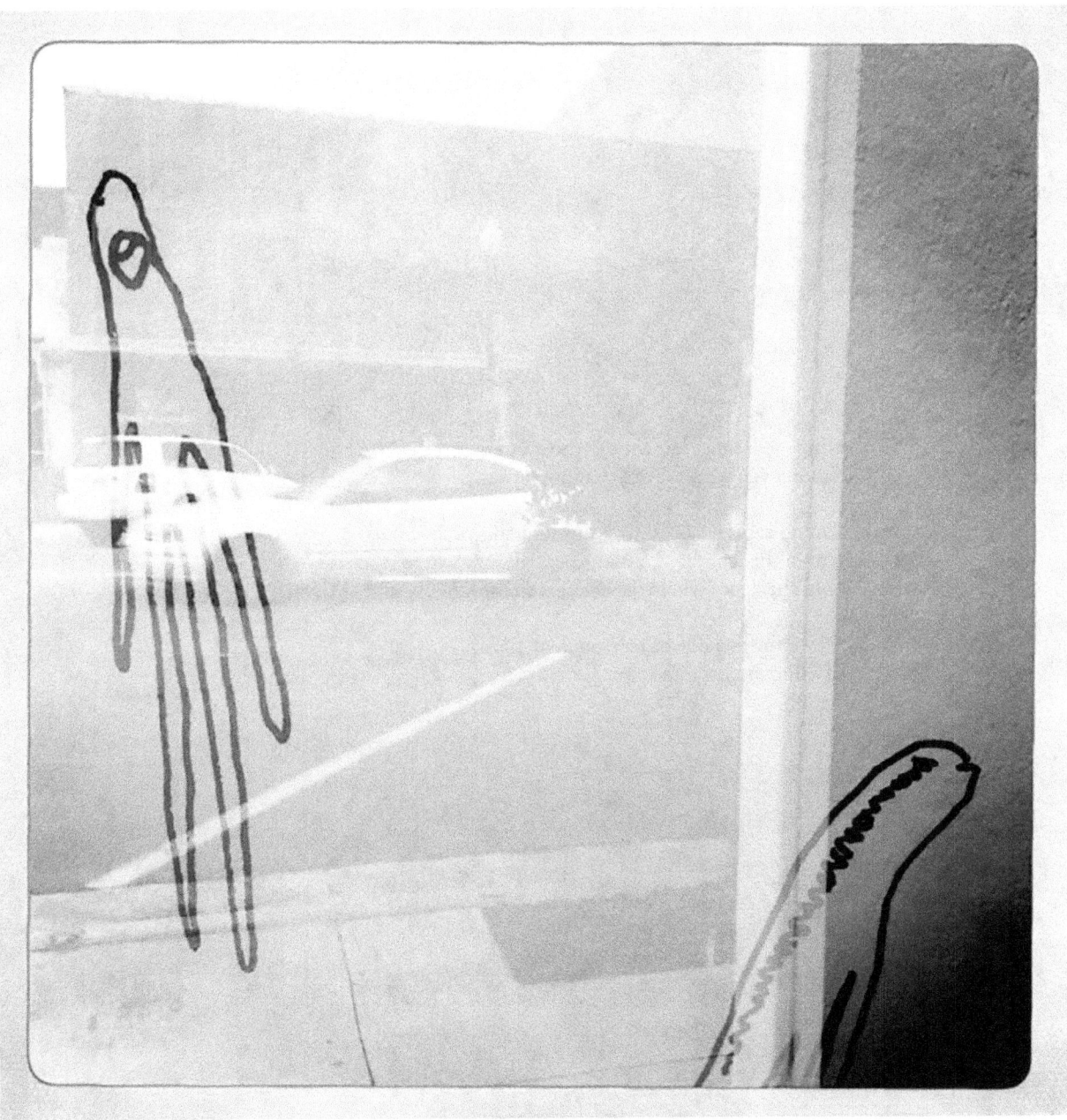

These reds, in the gravity, in the hair around the lake
around your head/heart, shadow tresses.

I'm up early, for breakfast, and for you, god.
I'm in the long light, walking slowly, into where it starts,
into the depot where departure becomes.

I love the grenade of hair, opulent, born,
bearing me, over and over.

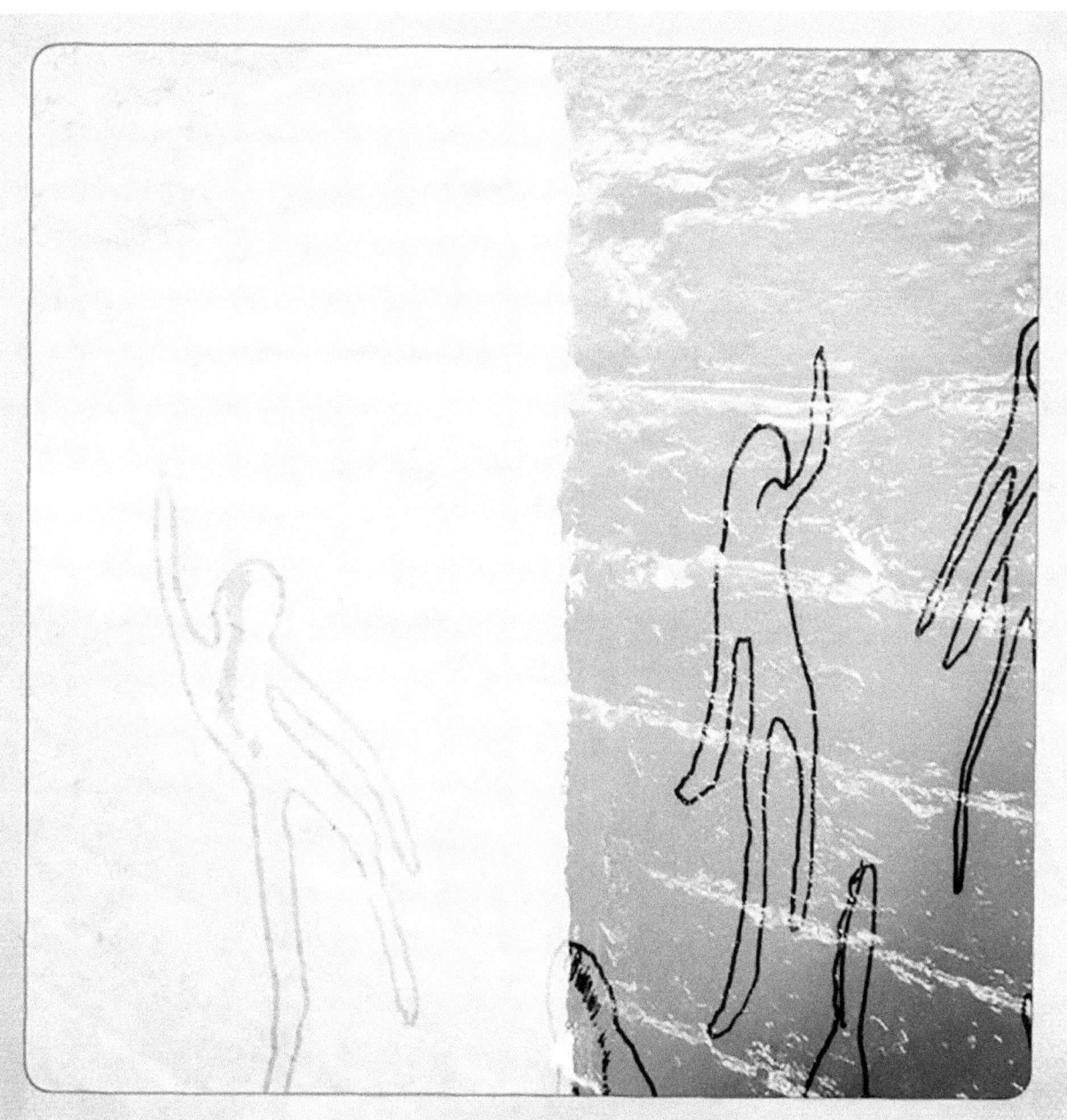

Spears in light, radiating from the traffic circle,
the sound of guitars, distorted perfectly into earth quake,
into gold, the weight of teeth, heavy inside
your head, lodging.

Bricks evaporate too, also, mortar sparks in secret
or the unobservable, like microscopic insects becoming
light, fire, fire, cherry bombs,
striking up, striking out, for you.

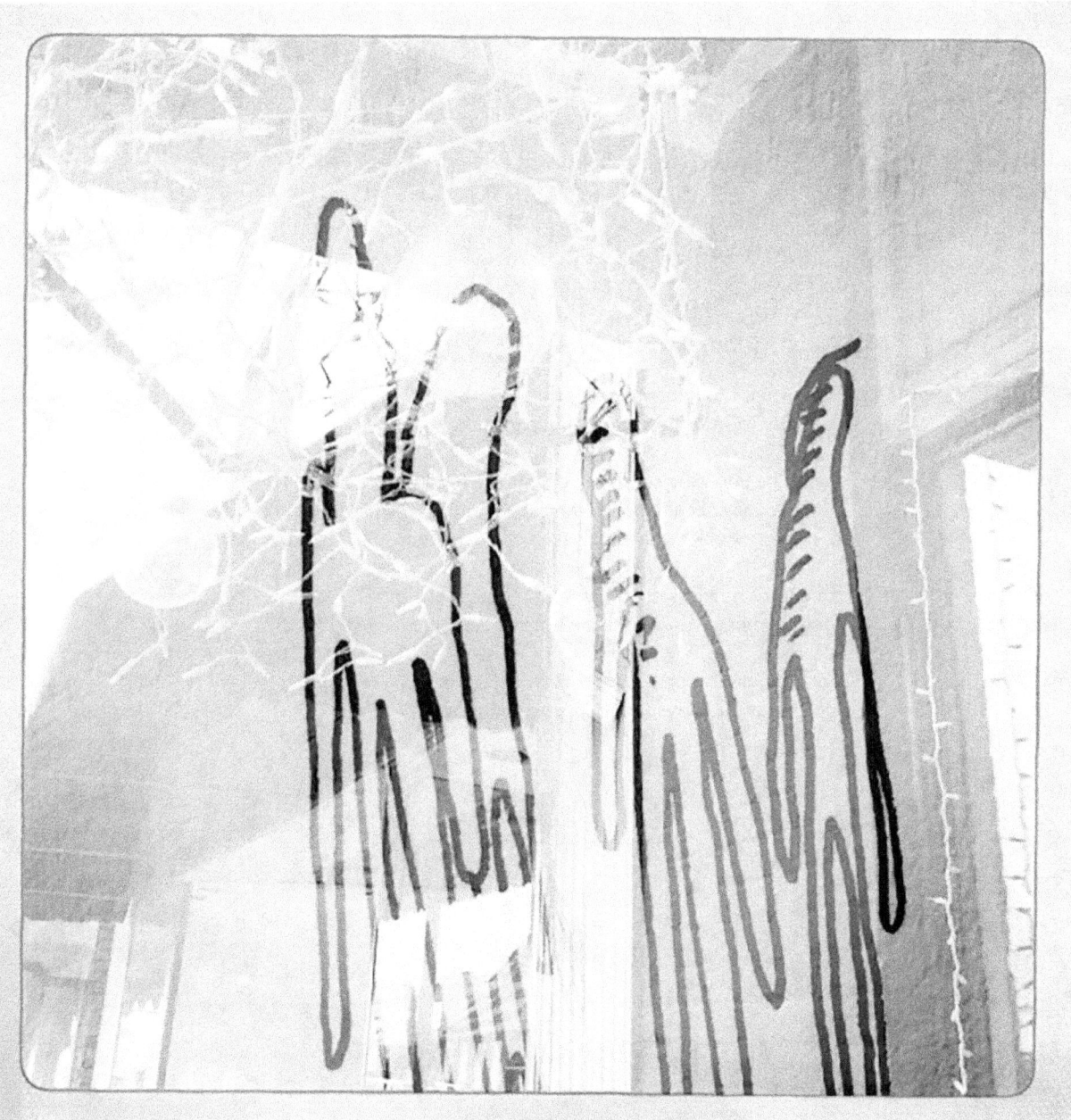

There ought to be a waterway if there is a town,
how else will the spirits arrive/depart.

Can it be upon the stars who circuit the night?
Or have they been confused for the gleaming headlights
of delivery trucks who are awake before the mosquito crowd?

This spirit inhabits my body for a moment as I pass,
for a moment I am a cricket's song remembered.

For a moment I am a cricket entwined in grass
looking at the heaven of an opened window.

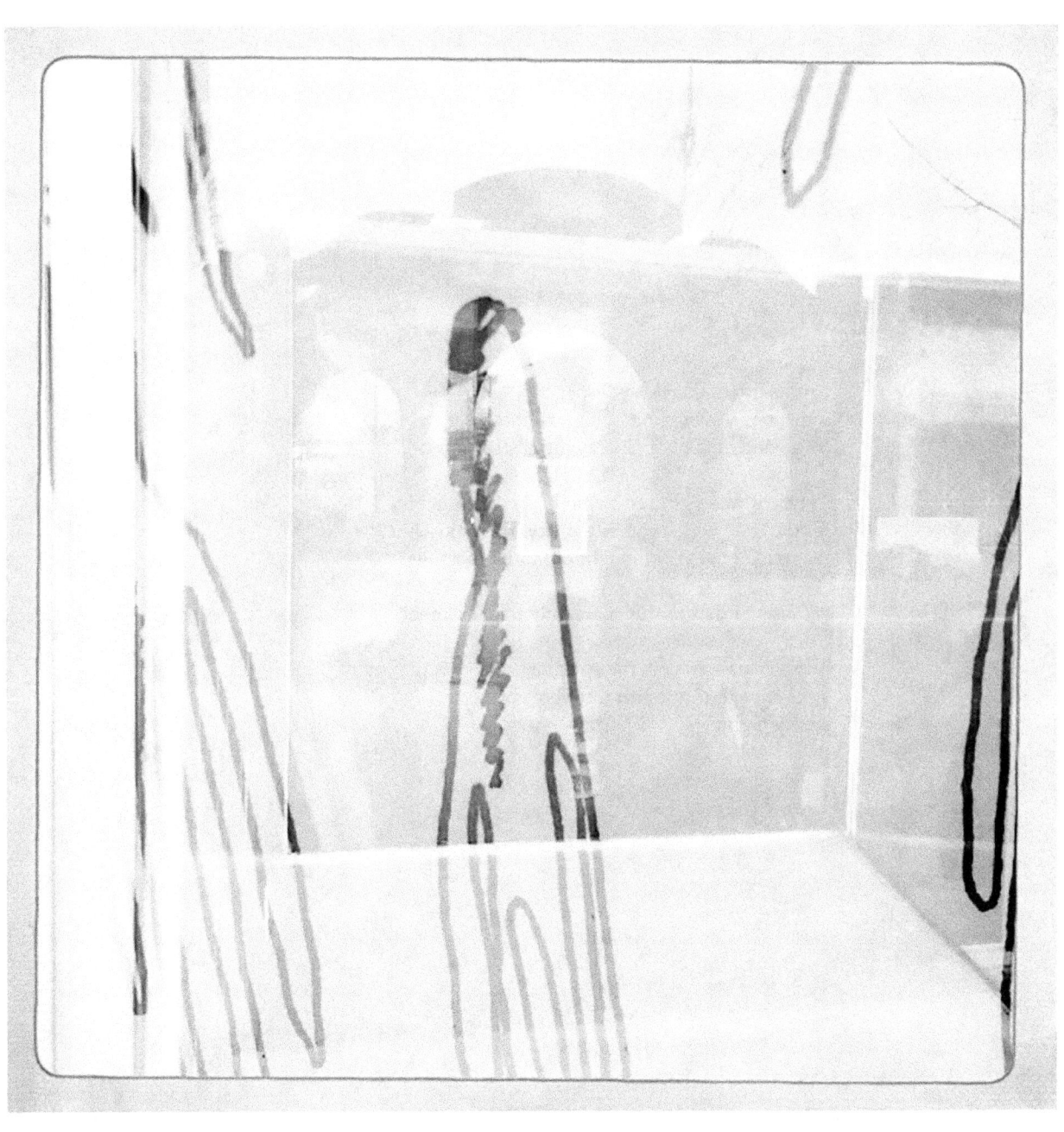

Listen, listen, there's a whisper. No,
someone's waving from a high window. No
it's a wind in the boughs caught in streetlight.

Maybe it was a girl resting on her wrist, searching
for the train which comes too late. The train
that makes the very thought of motion possible

because it exists in this space only for a moment.

The planets spiral on, the sycamore waves its thousand
arms enough to traverse the whole planet
once a night.

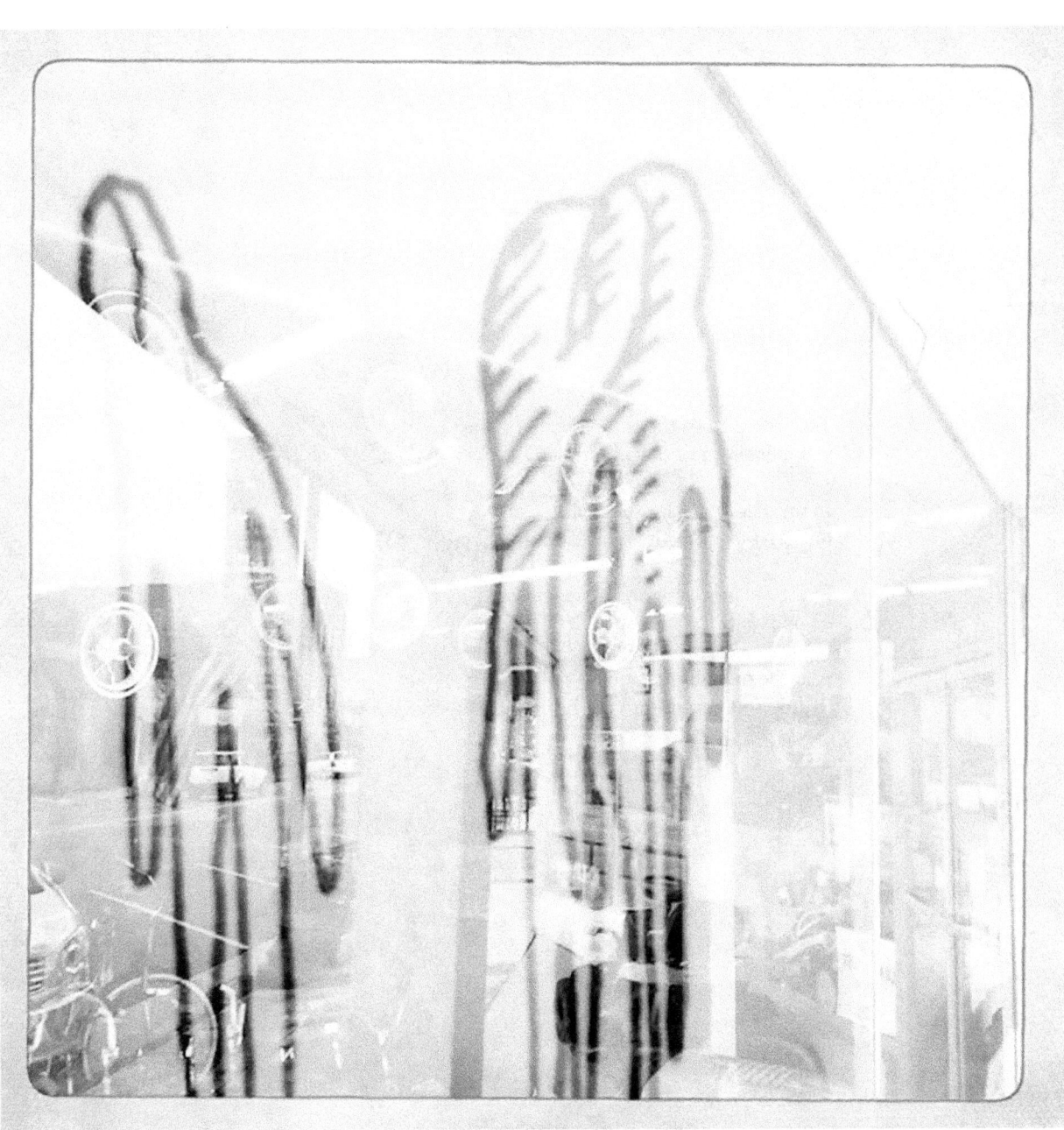

The first spirit in the church bell's ringing
will follow you until you turn left.

In the glass a distant sea is visible only,
the heart longs for it, but it is cold.

In the old grocery store, there are cold cuts
no one waits for, they stare.

And the moon waits outside for you
to drop some coins into her horizon.

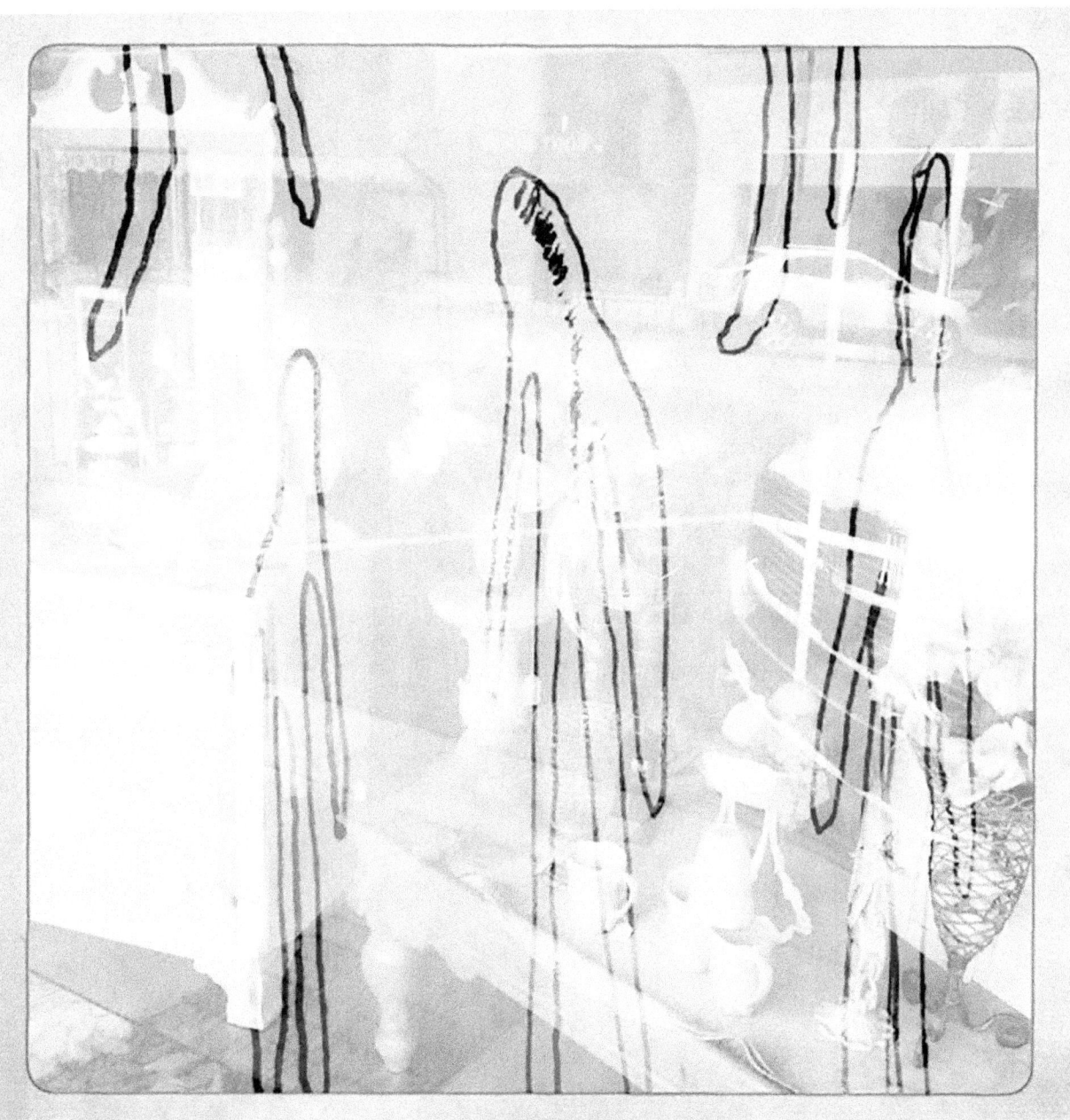

We were the color of red street signs,
of yellow traffic lights, of the temporary
oranges of road work warnings.

Some spirits are seasonal,
they return to your street corners
as though returning to life
after winter.

We radio each other when the peach trees
are heavy enough to pull on,
to pull us up when the bulbous meat comes
into the stars, hidden behind the orange glow above.

We were directional, pointing you around.

We return on a cold wind, when the time is right,
to make things still and warm.
You may notice, you may not
harvest anything they proffer.

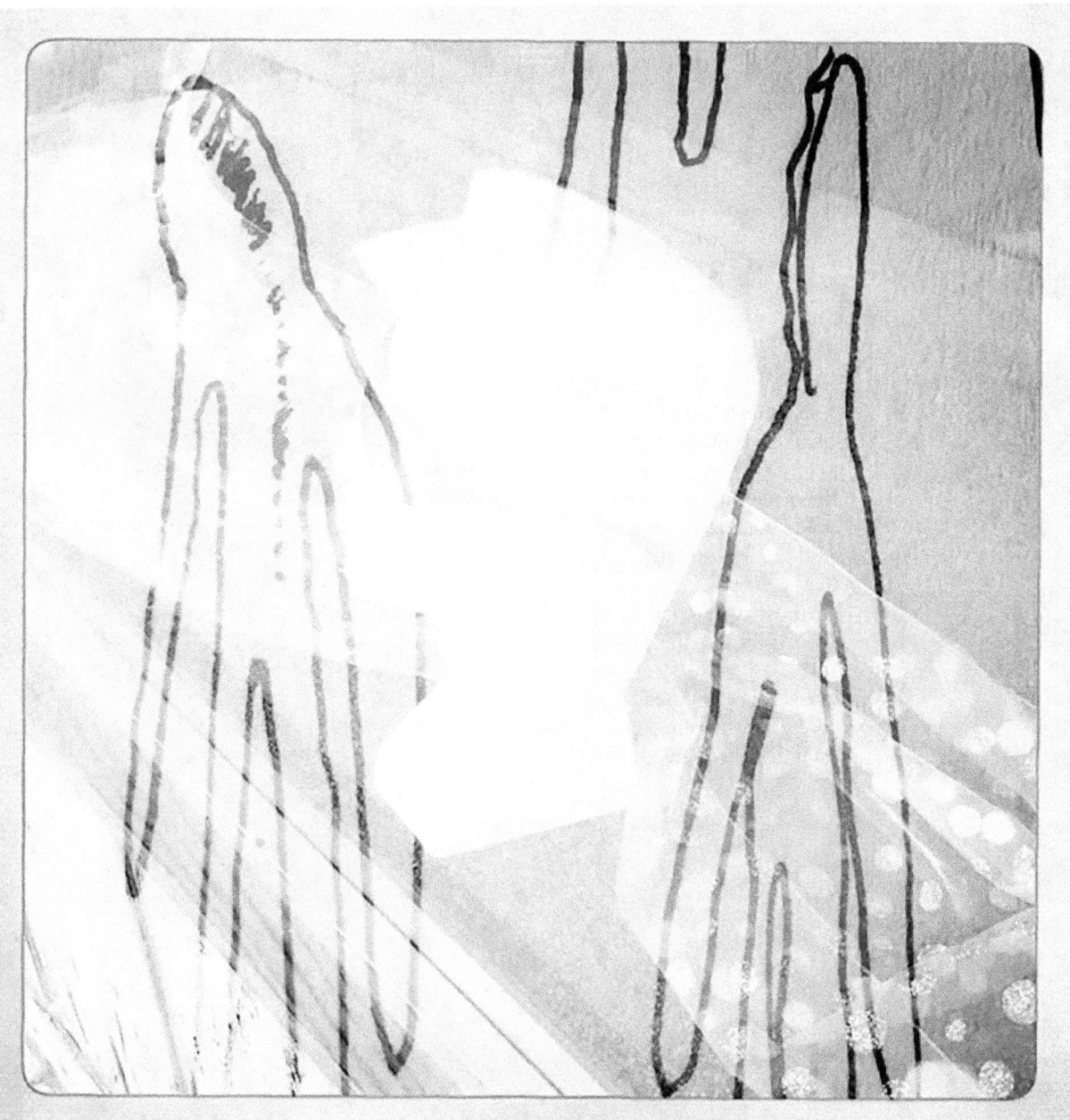

Even in town, the smoke drifts in
from the calming fires, reducing
the under growth and the shadow.

The cattle shift beside a church,
beside the fire. The smoke comes close,
inside your nostrils, caressing.

We dress and go out to turn
the corners, to parade in rich clothes,

and surrender to the licks of smoke, sweet pine
acrid plastic burning, unavoidable
reminders of where the borders are.

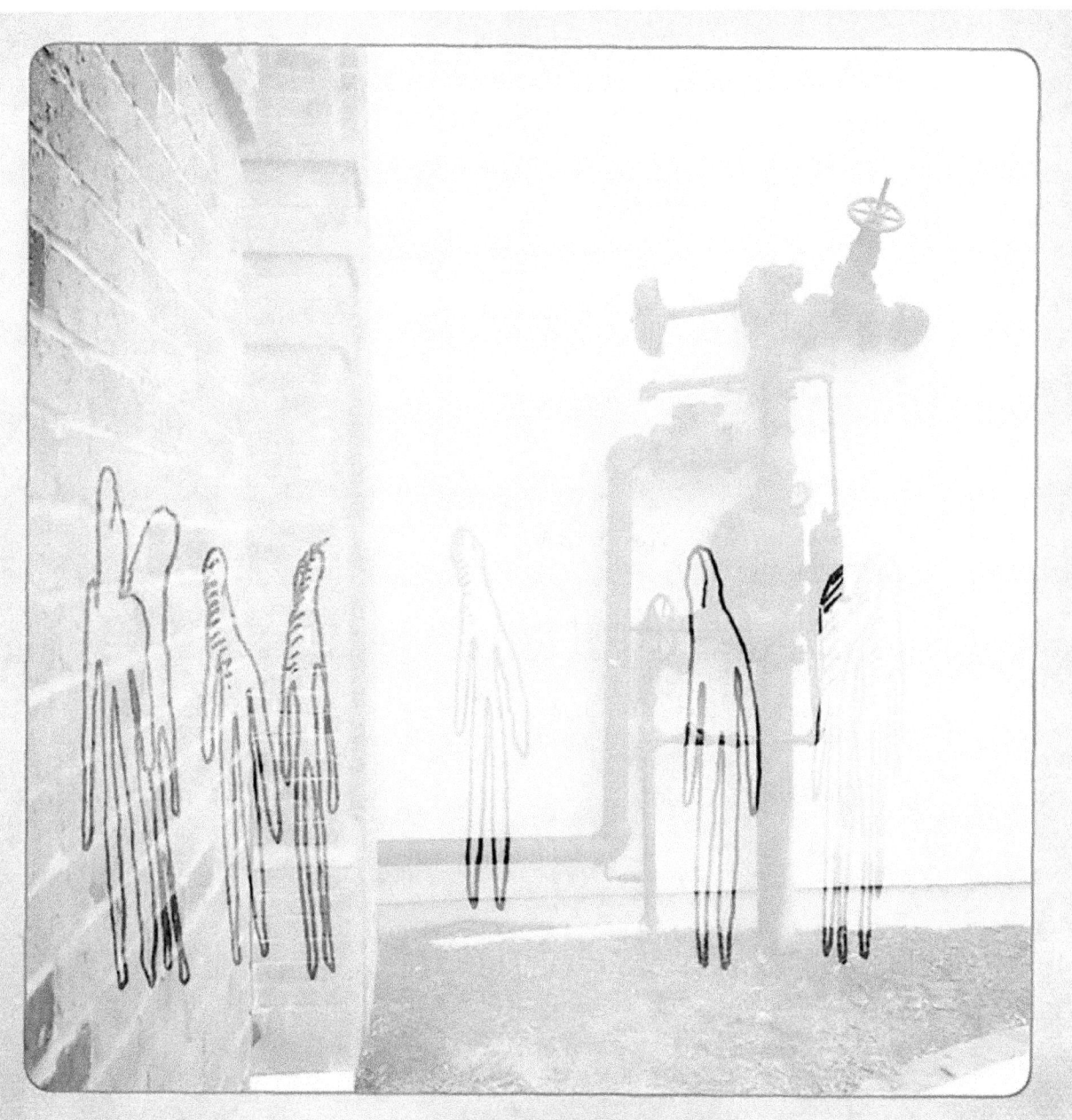

Shadow in silk, shadow in legs, shadow
in veins, shadow in the seam,

shadow in the mouth, shadow in hair
shadow consuming,

pulling in, pull me, tight.

Spirit left on the balcony, windows
open to the flutter.

The grocery is open, waiting to procure,
crates and rotten leaf lettuce,

the fields are growing fat, shadow, you can see
their secret ocean

from the spirit balcony.

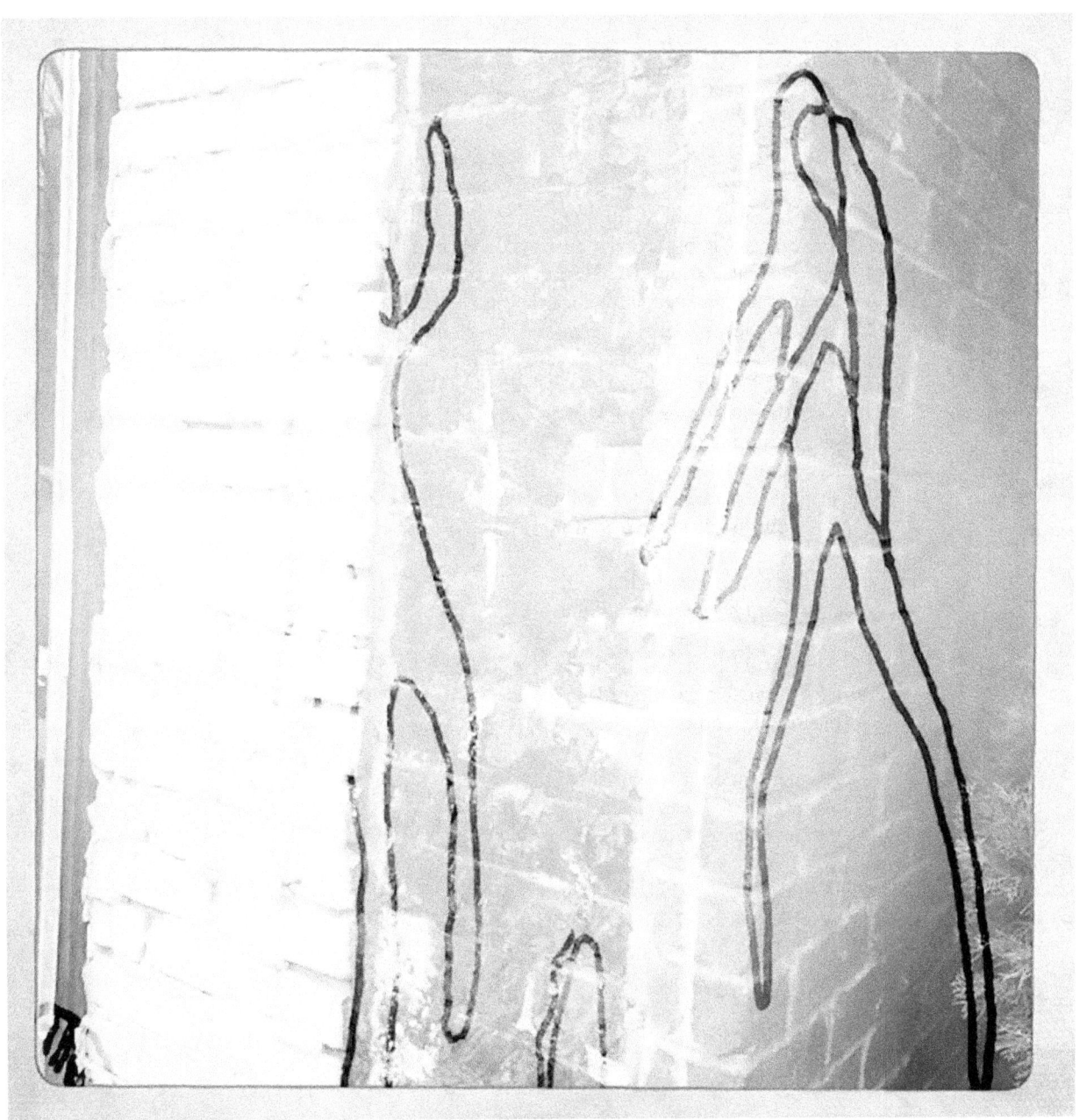

Poor spirit of math, of mirth,
unanswerable shade.
You carry a bag of incorrect answers, long vines
of errant calculations like a kudzu to cover
the roadside greenery and block the sun.
You carry a bag of insect wings and the sound
the eraser makes spreading the ashes of everything.

Take the shavings and make a pair of wings,
jump from the tall tower of division,
survey, on your way down, the correct
shape your errors made, mistaken geometry
that built this tower to leap from.

Spirits, remain for the longing,
the missed hearts, the thumping.

At night the birds are inspired
by the spirit's open mouths, soundless
moans taken up by the owl.

At noon, the fruit is nourished
by the need to be eaten. The vivid seed
puts a geometry around itself

In the end, every shape is a cage.

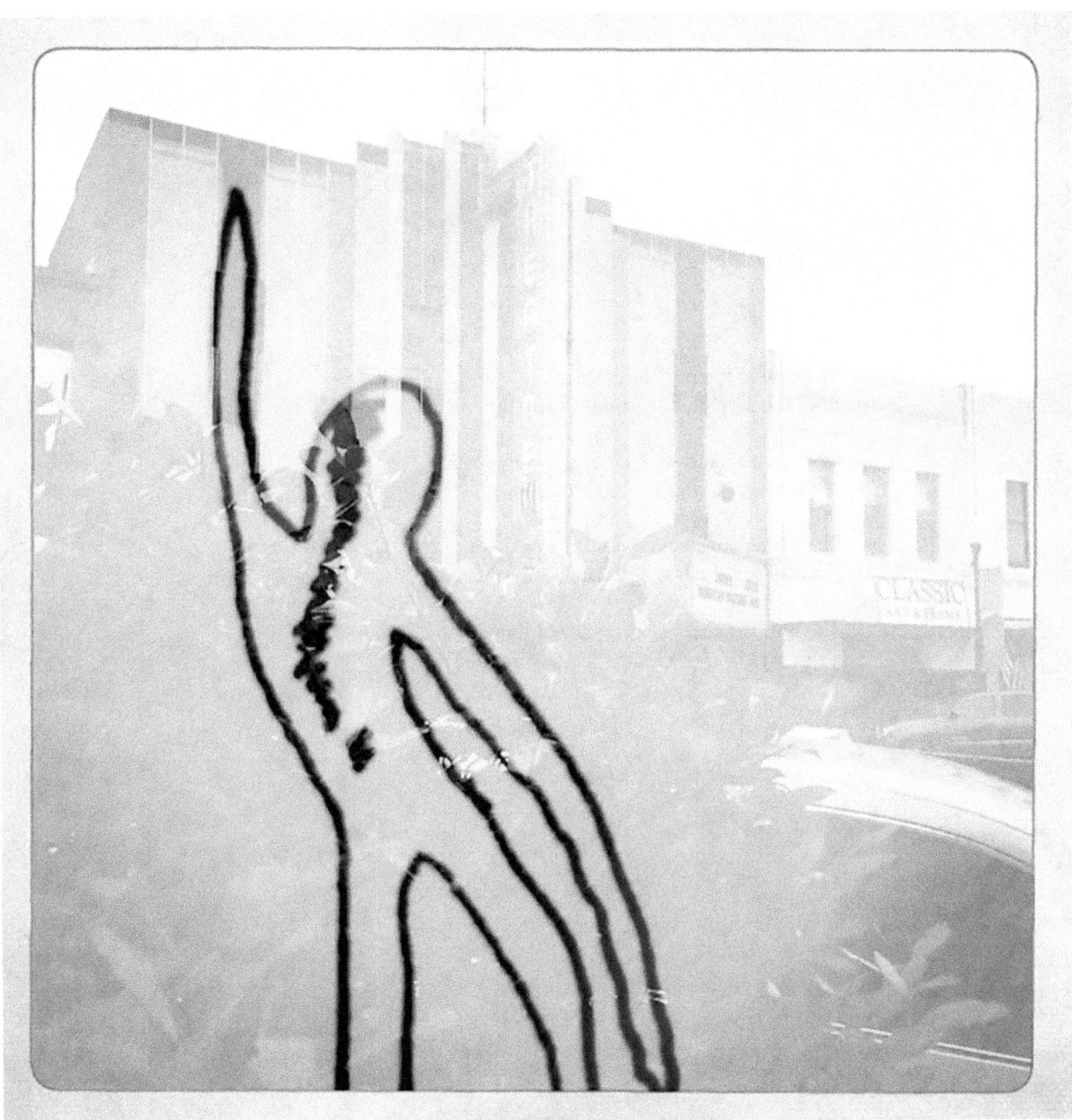

The flare of memory lures spirits
from the asphalt, fingertip by fingertip

as though a hand were entering your glove
of existence, taking shape, sprouting.

The winter streets do not want trees,
the cold sun sheds the prelude to warmth.

The summer street is a vacancy of light,
a shrewd glare invades the haze, spirit convection.

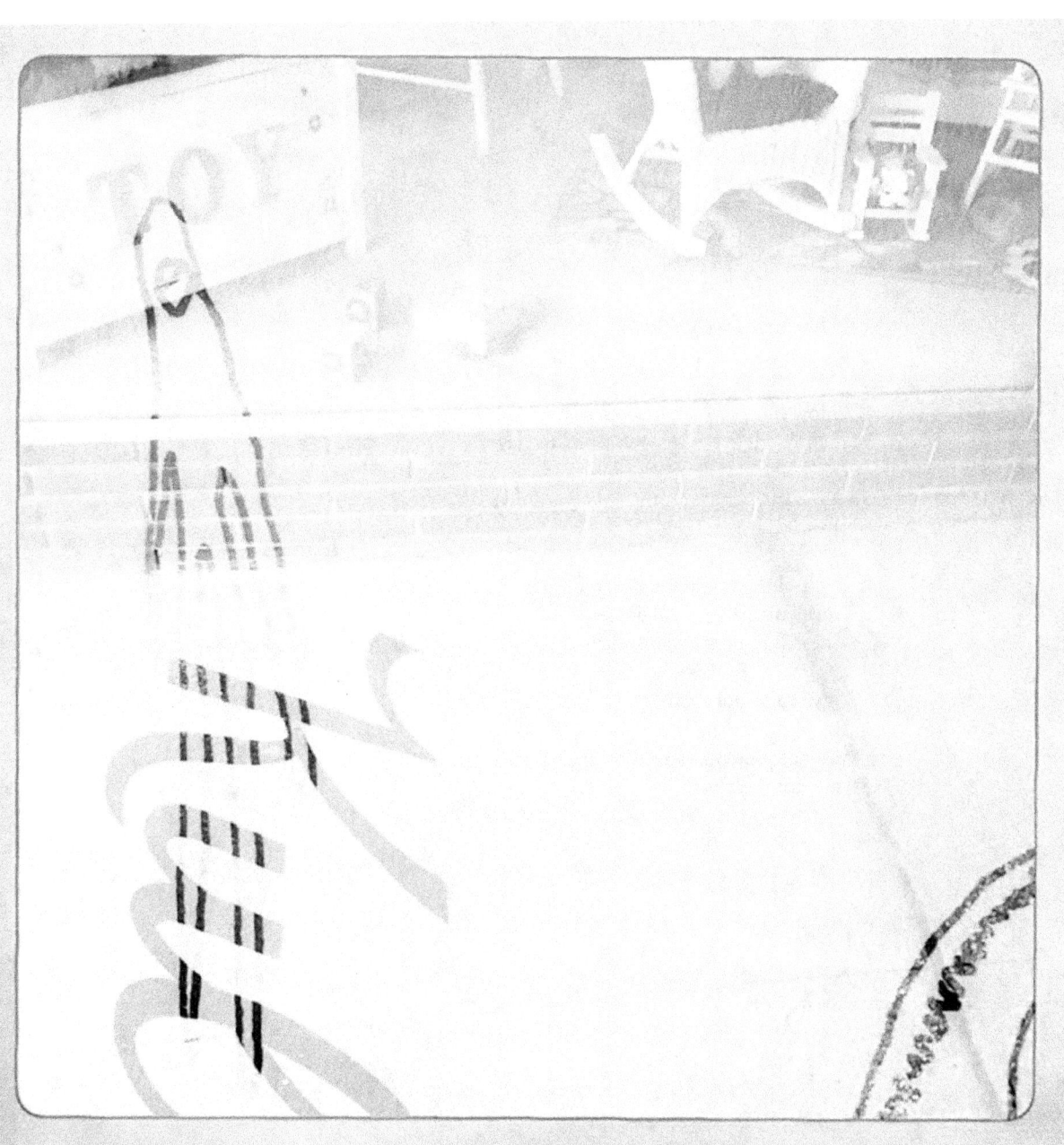

How much we are let in
to the ground, to gravy, gravitas.

How much you invited us to be
beholden, to be dragged from, to furlong.

We arrive, through the slits crumbled
from your masonry.

Spinning, we arrive in your cortex,
incalculable cerebral center,
these numbers invade, inevitable,

invited to domain
in your despair. These ghosts
do not pretend, permeate, their restrictions
are not dissolved.

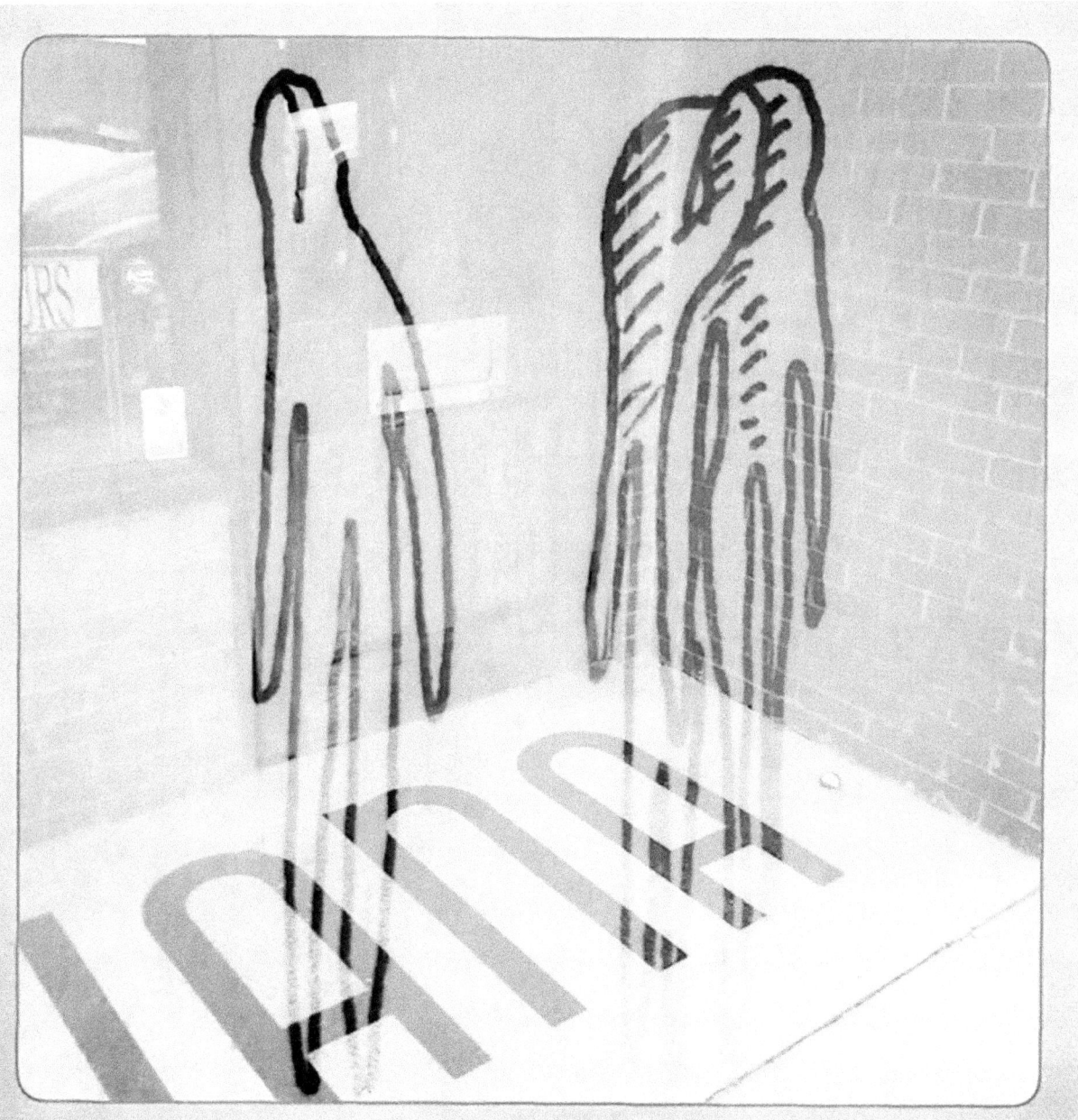

Corner me enough, popped lights
flashing, bulbs in the field, lily bright,

there must be a river. Not only the shop
front's reflection but my heart, growing long.

I'm exhausted from waiting and from the moon,
her slivers dropping, making me
gawk each time, night.

I'm innocent of words,
the river is inside me, sliding.

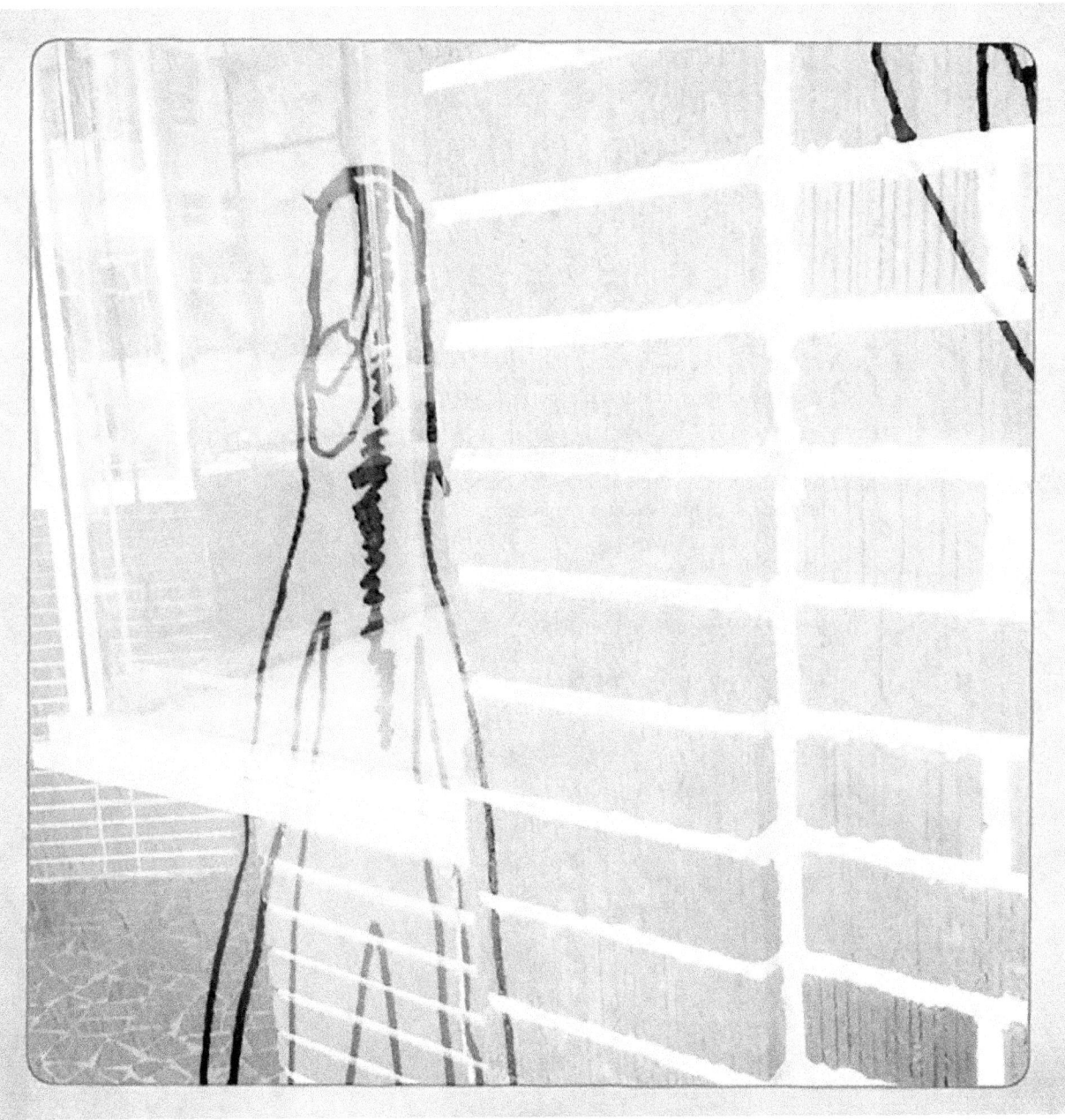

We collect the sounds of passing shadows.
We listen for its small creaks,
shoes and cloth and sidewalk scuffs.

Some of us move like wasps, floating
on ether, some of us cloud like smoke,
gusty and soft, lung-sponge expanding.

Some of us rise up on the walls,
like liquid glass, making way for you
as water does, displacing the path.

That's how we know you've been through
our skins.

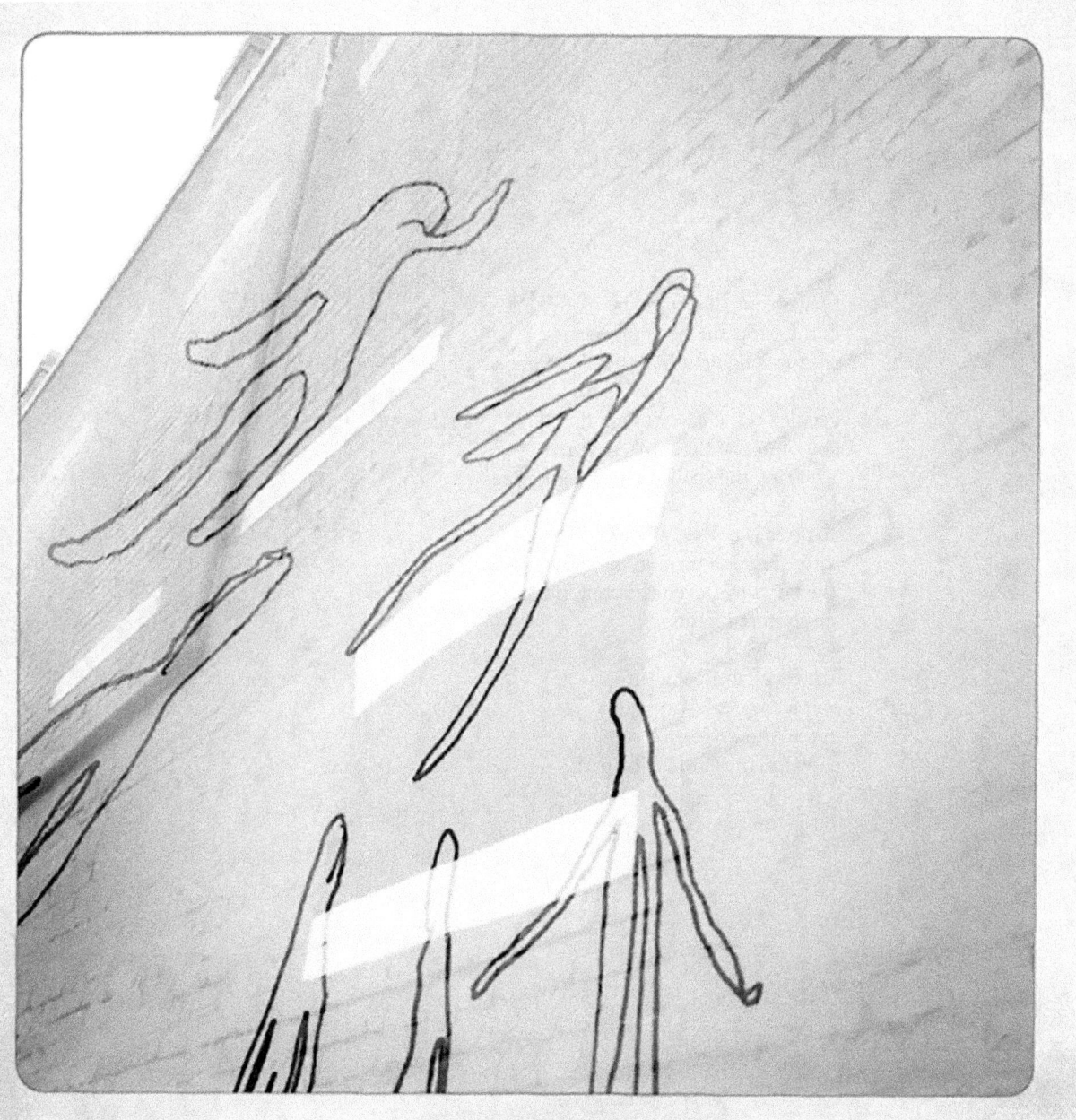

I have slept all afternoon
in the park. The bench is hard
but turns liquid when the blood pools.

People on their way to church
do not notice the lord's children
acquiring the shade of a morning tree.

The tree is not yet a house,
nature is not a turning into.
The buildings, even the church herself,
are confused nature.

The bent fabric of a shroud
over a corpse. My body
in the immobile, stretched
between, the land of the park.

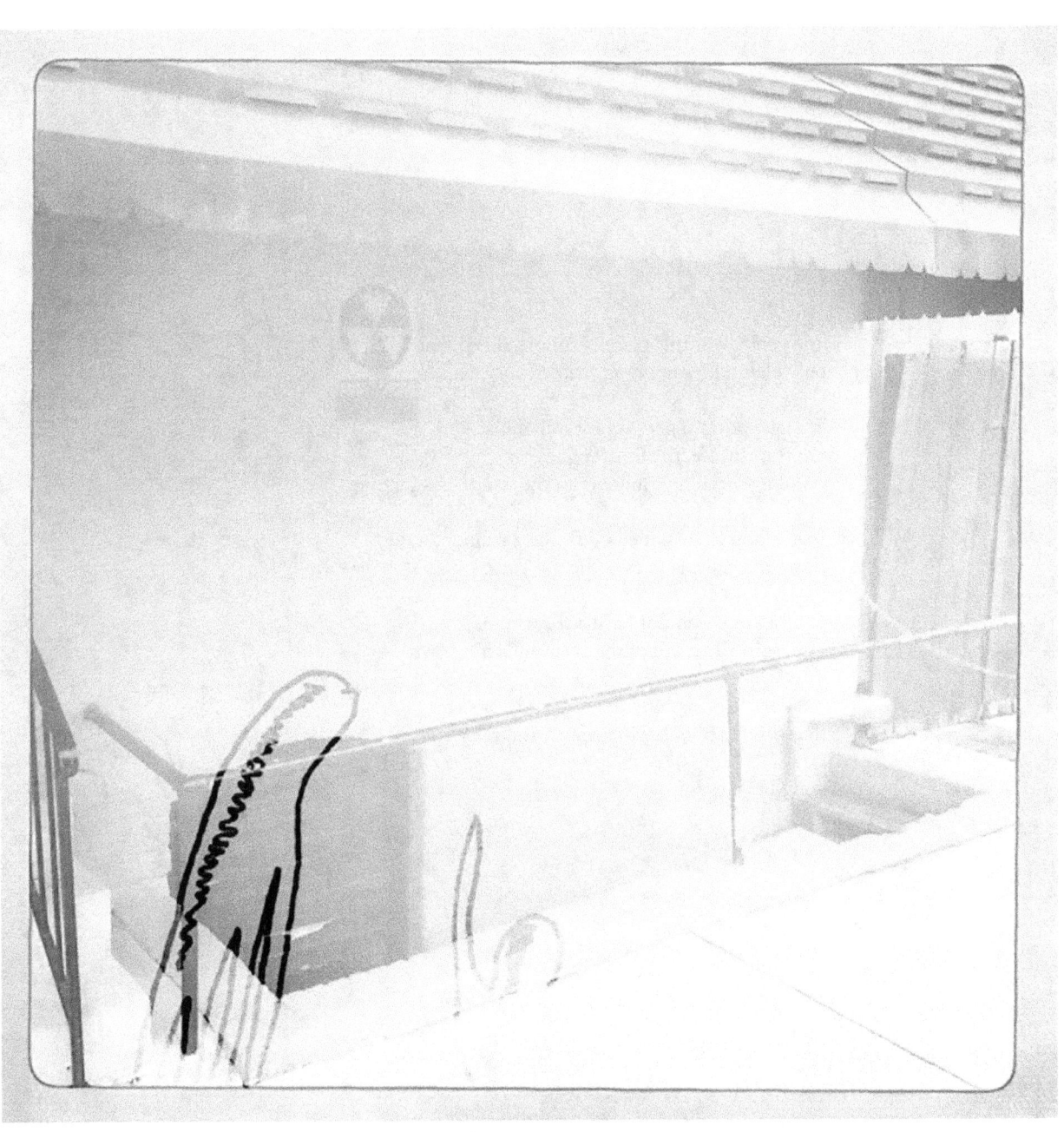

The geology of this place is simple, no cliff, no hill,
only plains. Flat noise on the drifting plain.

The sear of train goes on for millennia.
On this surface, the rooster goes on
invading mornings, more than the wind, invalidating.

I am rising to imagined cliffs like a balloon,
rising in an airplane over the flat earth

to jump out. I do not have a parachute.
I am spirit. The will of the river pulls me down.

She makes everything flat, she and her sister
the wind. I am half wind, spirit, and river

bound to current.

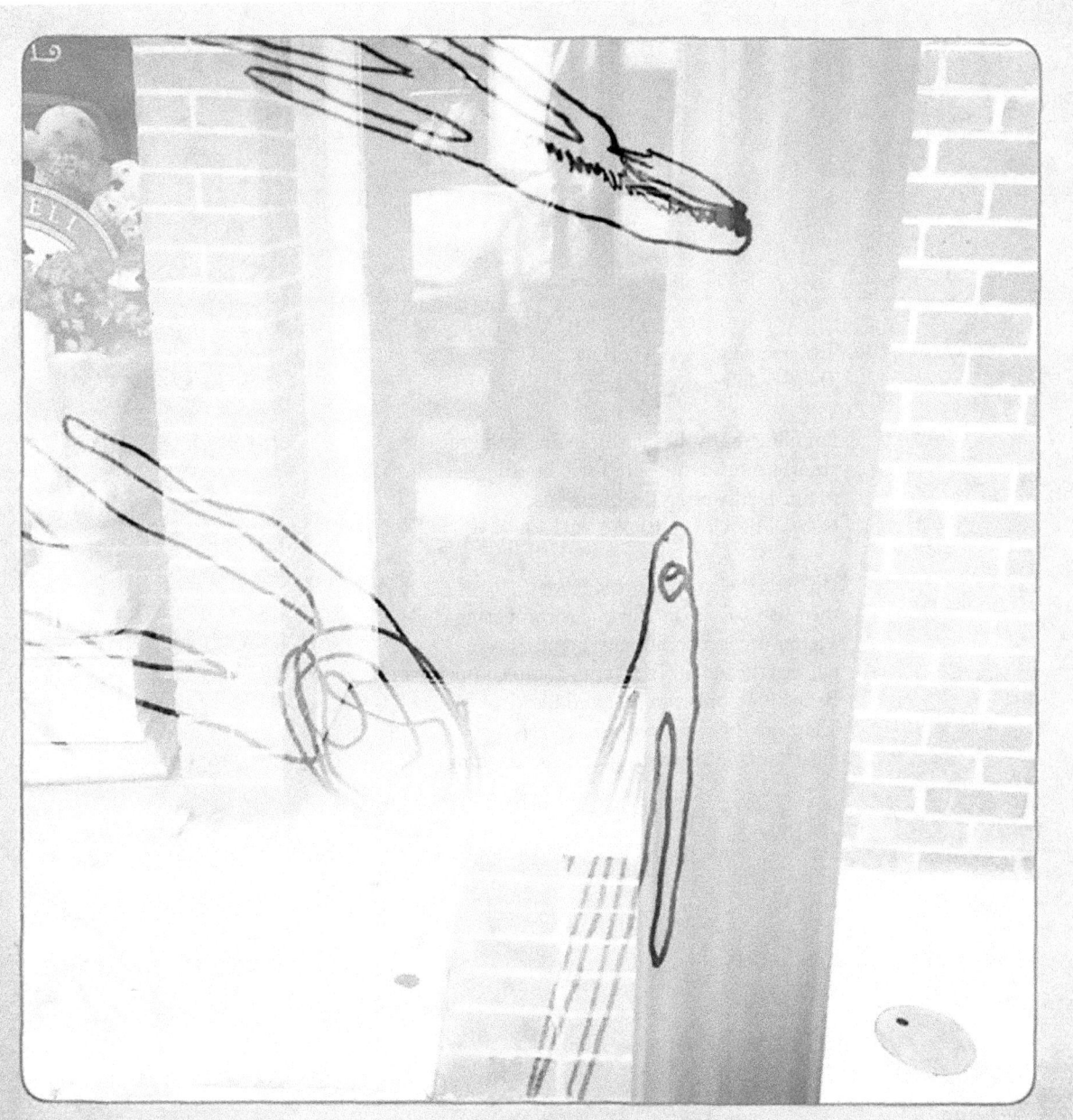

The stained glass is incorrect.
There is no country of rock.

I'm filling out your questionnaire as the sun
absorbs me. I'm not sure I will be able
to finish answering the questions
before I have to go back.

Up here, the creatures recognize us,
their fish tails swat. The tree is composing
a letter of disappointment. Stand
tall together, men. The stones are unconscious still.
Beneath us, only summer and flies.
These are the windows, stained glass
pillars, fragile as wrists, holding everything up.

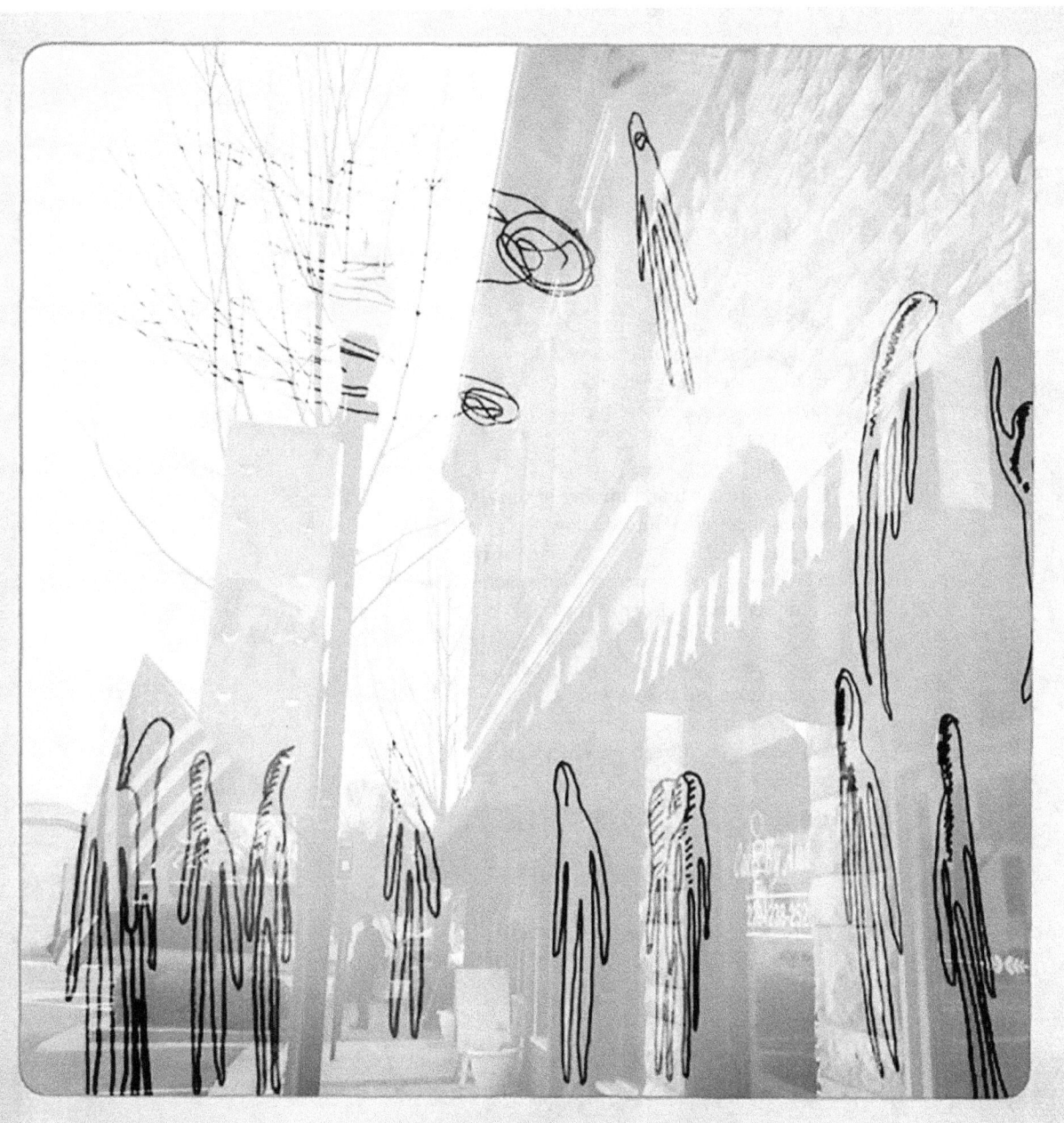

Spirit women in stockings. Drainpipes
lay down on the storefront necks,
wired smiles fuse the cracks.
Their eyes are full of fruit, piles
of fruit tumbling out.

The lost are dancing. Jumping in the air,
balling themselves into shadow
and leaf dark. The street is the largest river
in creation. The lost are baptizing each other
all the way down, as far as they can go.

Palsy fabric and end tables. This town
is antique only, only the wind's home.
The grass cuts back at feet, defensive
and armed. The insects are shell shocked
crushed by summer, trod.

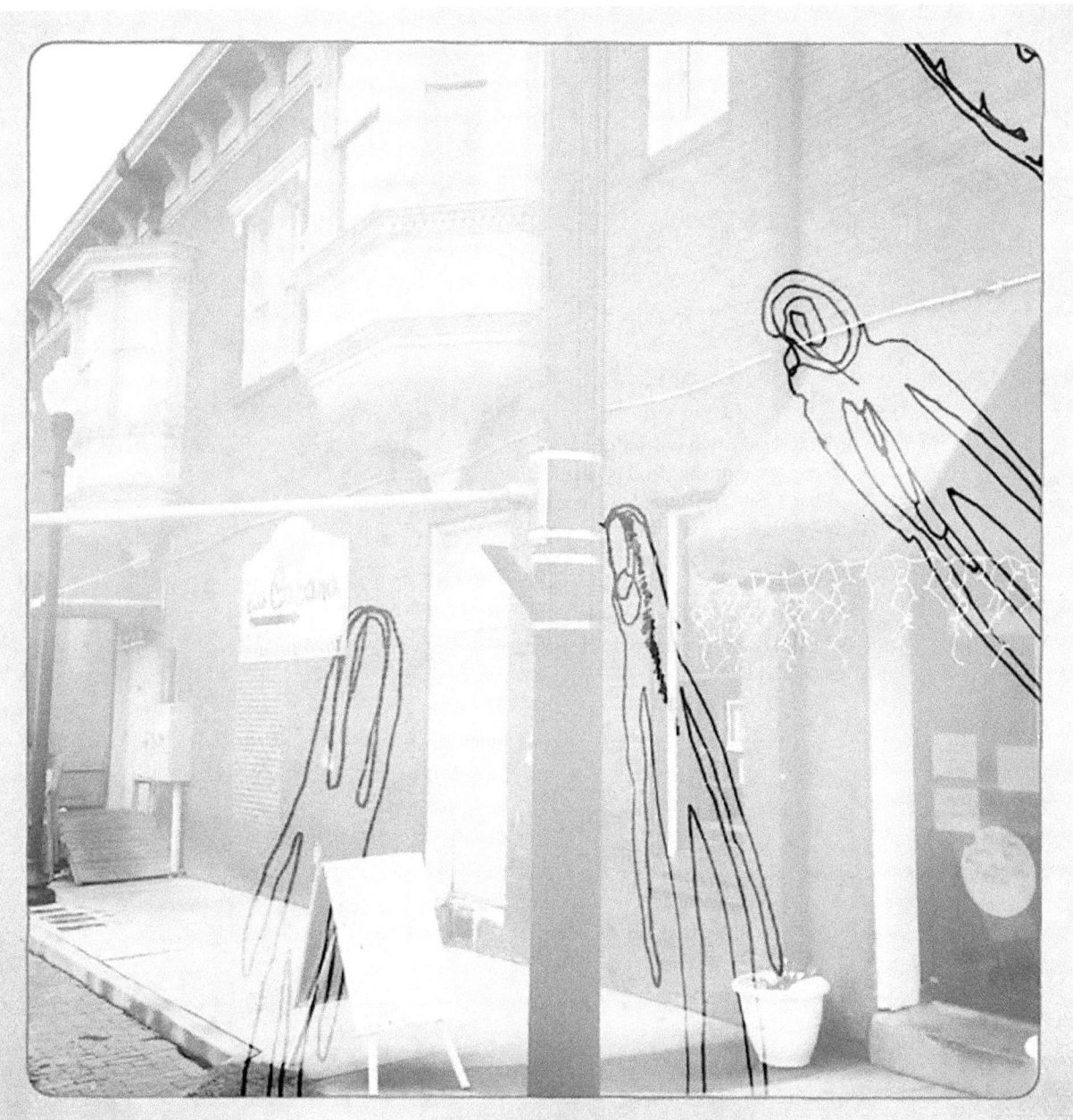

What dead town has no music?
What town of the dead is silent?
What steel is unmoved, what rail doesn't sing?
What theater is not full
of ghosts, of smoke and pianoforte,
of drizzle and dust and diesel
exhaust? Everything is singing
a birthday song, a dirge on the river,
crops and lament.

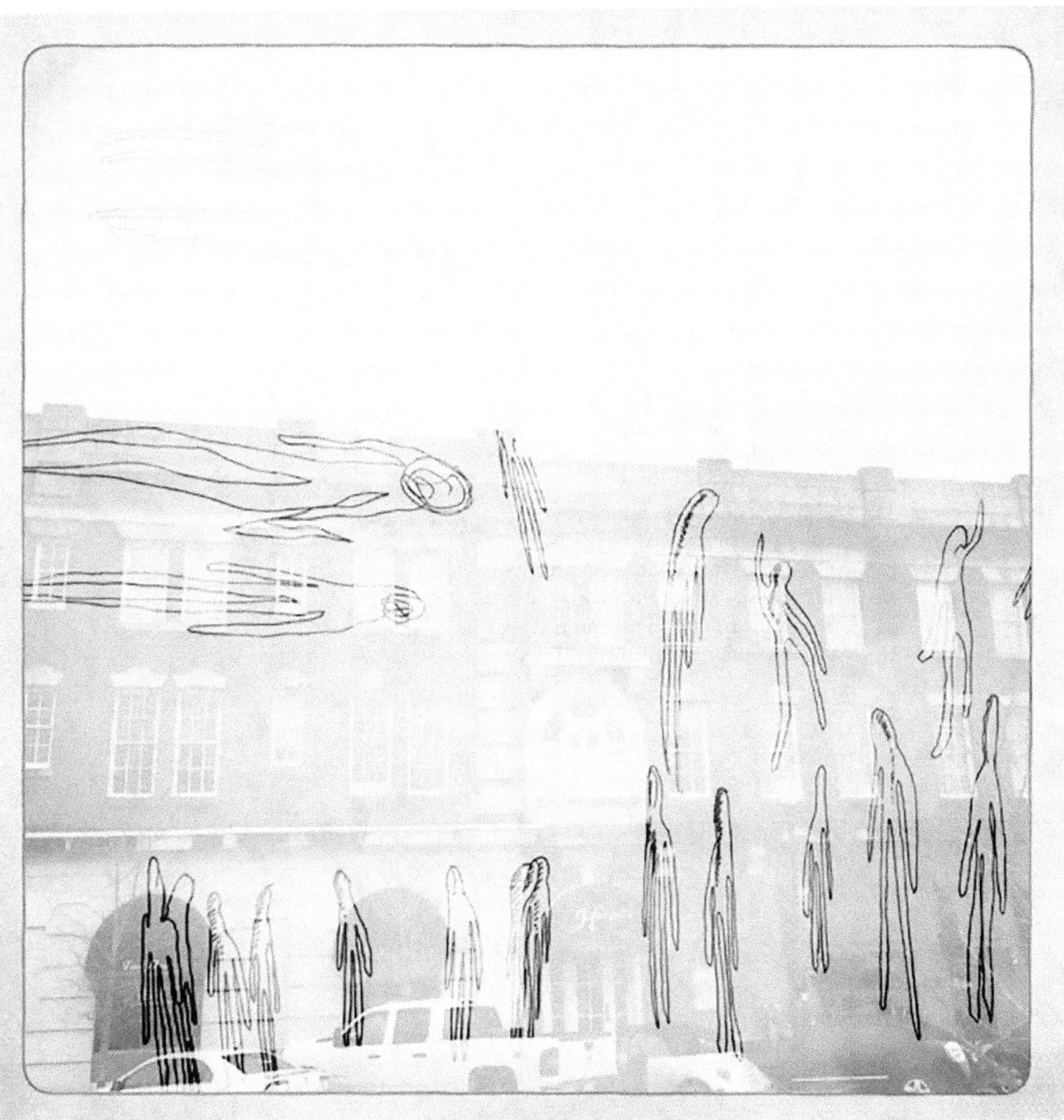

Naked brick, naked peaches,
naked sidewalk. Unashamed
and synthetic. Naked mornings.

The empty fountain is broken,
no water. Unashamed and gallant,
gaunt, the bronze, the ladies accept
the grey sky, accept the water,
accept the fruit. And the mortised corner,
angelic, becomes gaslight, drifting.

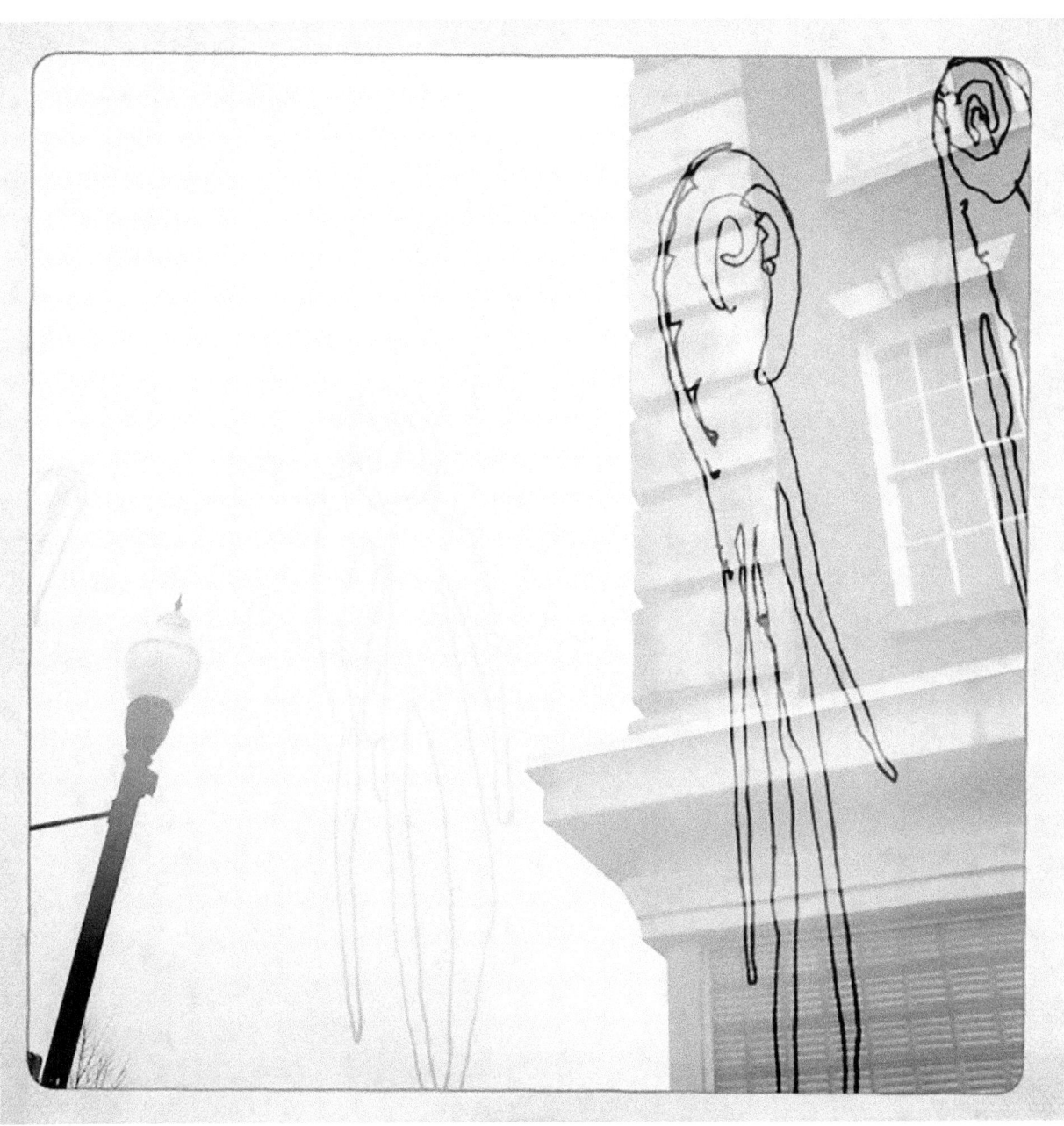

SPECTRALS
IN
OMEGA

www.ingramcontent.com/pod-product-compliance
Lightning Source LLC
Chambersburg PA
CBHW080605180526
45168CB00007B/2787